The Library of PIRATES™

Blackbeard

Eighteenth-Century Pirate of the Spanish Main and Carolina Coast

Aileen Weintraub

The Rosen Publishing Group's
PowerKids Press™
New York

To my DaddyMonster, who was the most fearless of them all

Published in 2002 by The Rosen Publishing Group, Inc.
29 East 21st Street, New York, NY 10010

First Edition

Book design: Michael Caroleo and Michael de Guzman
Project Editors: Jennifer Landau, Jennifer Quasha
Consultant: Ken Kinkor

Photo credits: pp. 4 (Blackbeard), 12 (pirate illustration) © The Granger Collection; pp. 11 (gold bullion), 12 (treasure chest), 16 (top), 16 (bottom) © Christie's Images Ltd.; p. 11 (gun and cutlass) © National Maritime Museum Picture Gallery; p. 11 (wine bottles) © Diane Hardy, N.C. Archives and History; p. 4 (map) © Michael Maslan Historic Photographs/CORBIS; p. 7 ship illustration by Jean Boudriot, (treasure chest) © Index Stock; pp. 8, 15, 19 illustrations by Mica Angela Fulgium; p. 12 (treasure map) created by Michael Caroleo and Michael de Guzman; p. 16 (map of N.C.) © MapArt; p. 20 © SuperStock.

Weintraub, Aileen, 1973–
    Blackbeard: eighteenth century pirate of the Spanish main and Carolina coast / Aileen Weintraub
    —1st ed.
        p. cm. — (The library of pirates)
    Includes bibliographical references and index.
    ISBN 0–8239–5794–2 (lib. bdg.)
1. Teach, Edward, d. 1718—Juvenile literature. 2. Pirates—North Carolina—Atlantic Coast—Biography—Juvenile literature. 3. Pirates—Virginia—Atlantic Coast—Biography—Juvenile literature. 4. Atlantic Coast (N.C.)—History—18th century—Juvenile literature. 5. Atlantic Coast (Va.)—History—18th century—Juvenile literature. 6. North Carolina—History—Colonial period, ca. 1600–1775—Juvenile Literature. 7. Virginia—History—Colonial period, ca. 1600–1775—Juvenile literature. [1. Blackbeard, d. 1718. 2. Pirates.]
I. Title.
    F257.T422 W45 2002
    975'.5'02—dc21

                                                                00-011240

Manufactured in the United States of America

Contents

Blackbeard may have sailed as a pirate as early as 1714.

The Golden Age of Piracy

The pirate known as Blackbeard was one of the most feared pirates of all time. Blackbeard was born in Bristol, England, about 1680. Most historians think his real name was Edward Teach. Not much is known about Blackbeard's early life. Records show that he started out as a **privateer**, or a man who worked for the government, legally **plundering** enemy ships. Instead of payment, privateers kept part of the treasure they stole.

Blackbeard lived during the Golden Age of Piracy. This was a time during the early 1700s when European countries claimed land in North and South America. Many trade ships sailed to **foreign** countries. European navies were not big enough to protect the seas from robbers seeking treasure and fortune.

The *Queen Anne's Revenge*

Blackbeard worked as a privateer for a man named Benjamin Hornigold. In 1716, Blackbeard helped Hornigold capture ships full of **booty**. He tired of being a privateer, however, and did not want to work for the government any longer. Blackbeard took command of the *Concorde*, a French slave ship that he and Hornigold had captured. The ship had been captured near the island of St. Vincent's in the Caribbean. It had three masts and was 90 feet (27.4 m) long. Blackbeard renamed the *Concorde* the *Queen Anne's Revenge*. This ship could store more than 300 tons (272 t) of booty and could hold up to 250 pirates. Soon Blackbeard had at least three other ships and almost 400 pirates under his command.

Pirates had to hide the fact that they were sailing in pirate ships so that they could get close enough to their enemies.

Blackbeard braided his hair as well as his beard.

A Fearsome Pirate

Blackbeard **terrorized** the high seas from 1716 to 1718. During that time, he captured dozens of ships. He did much of his raiding along the coast of North Carolina, South Carolina, and Virginia. Blackbeard stole gold, silver, **pieces of eight**, weapons, medicine, food, and rum. He became known as an evil and dangerous man.

Blackbeard got his nickname because of his long, dark hair and beard. He braided his beard and tied it with ribbons. Before attacking a ship, Blackbeard would tie slow-burning **fuses** to his hair. These fuses made it look as though smoke was coming out of his head. Seeing a "smoking man" about to attack made Blackbeard's enemies fear him.

Taking over a City

In May 1718, Blackbeard set sail for North Carolina to ask the governor, Charles Eden, for a **pardon**. Blackbeard was thinking of giving up his criminal activities. He could not give up his life as a pirate, though. Instead he ended up blocking off the port in Charleston, South Carolina. He lined up his ships along the harbor so that no one could get in or out of the city. Blackbeard held the entire city of Charleston for **ransom**! Blackbeard wouldn't leave until his demands were met. He wanted money, supplies, and medicine. Blackbeard and his men blocked the port for weeks. Finally the city gave in to Blackbeard's demands. He got exactly what he wanted without a single shot being fired from either side.

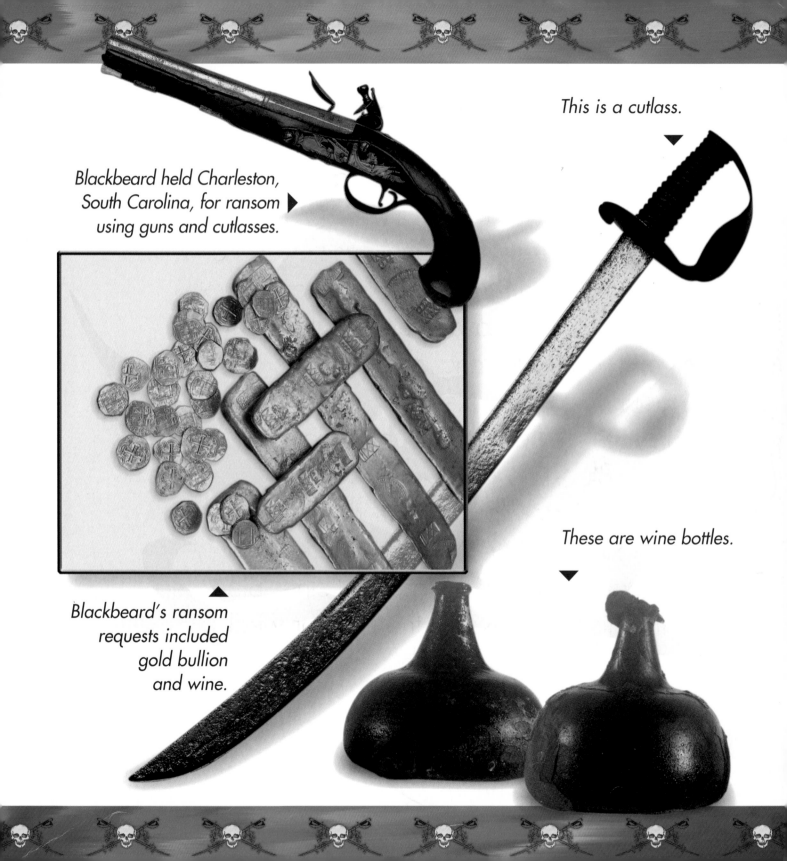

This is a cutlass. ▼

Blackbeard held Charleston, South Carolina, for ransom using guns and cutlasses. ▶

Blackbeard's ransom requests included gold bullion and wine. ▲

These are wine bottles. ▼

No one is sure what happened
to Blackbeard's treasure.

Blackbeard Betrays His Crew

In June 1718, Blackbeard's ship was full of treasure from the attack on Charleston, South Carolina. Blackbeard had a plan to cheat his crew out of the booty. He secretly took all the booty off the *Queen Anne's Revenge* and hid it on one of his smaller ships. Then he ran the *Queen Anne's Revenge* **aground** and made it look like an accident. Everyone thought that the treasure was lost with the ship.

Blackbeard took his favorite crew members and sailed off on his smaller ship with the hidden booty. He left 25 crew members on a deserted island. Stede Bonnet, another man that Blackbeard had **betrayed**, finally saved the men **marooned** on the island.

Hardships on the High Seas

Many people think of a pirate's life as exciting and full of adventure. In reality, pirates lived dangerous lives. Blackbeard and his crew probably faced times of hardship. They might not have had much food or money between attacks. Pirates often suffered from scurvy, a disease caused by a lack of vitamin C in a person's diet. Scurvy can cause bleeding gums, bruises on the skin, and even death.

Blackbeard needed fast ships to catch up with his enemies and surprise them. This meant he had to keep his ships in good condition on seas that were often stormy. He also had to have a lot of weapons and needed to be prepared for battle.

Keeping ships in good condition required a lot of work from pirates. ▶

North Carolina

It is thought that Blackbeard shared his treasure with Governor Charles Eden of North Carolina.

A Pirate's Secret Deal

Being a pirate was illegal. Many pirates were put to death for their crimes. However, some pirates had secret agreements with governments or wealthy people. A wealthy person might give a pirate money for a journey. In return the pirate agreed to split any treasure that he stole. Blackbeard became a secret partner with Governor Charles Eden of North Carolina. Eden gave Blackbeard protection.

It was also easy for pirates to get pardons for their crimes. A pirate could offer money to a government official so that the official would ignore the pirate's bad deeds. Governments often were willing to forgive a pirate for his criminal activities and let him live freely if he promised not to attack any ships. Blackbeard received a pardon from Governor Eden.

A Battle to the Death

Even after Blackbeard received a pardon from Governor Eden, he did not stop plundering ships. Governor Alexander Spotswood of Virginia feared that Blackbeard and other pirates were going to use an island in Ocracoke, North Carolina, as a meeting place. Spotswood offered money to anyone who could capture Blackbeard. He sent ships to look for him. In November 1718, Lieutenant Robert Maynard from England's Royal Navy spotted Blackbeard. Maynard tricked the pirate into coming onto his ship. Blackbeard wasn't ready for an attack. After the two men fought with swords, Maynard pulled out a gun. Finally, one of Maynard's men cut off Blackbeard's head.

Historians learn about piracy through logbooks, trial documents, and reports from governors.

Blackbeard and eight of his men died
during the fight with Maynard.

Legends of Blackbeard

Many **legends** surround the life and death of the most feared pirate on the high seas. After Lieutenant Robert Maynard and his crew killed Blackbeard, they threw his body overboard. It is said that Blackbeard's body swam around the ship several times before drowning. Another legend about Blackbeard is that he had 14 wives.

Today nobody is even sure what Blackbeard looked like. He is usually shown in pictures as a mean-looking man with smoke coming out of his head. One thing is certain about Blackbeard. His death marked the beginning of the end of the Golden Age of Piracy.

An Amazing Discovery

Few sunken pirate ships have ever been recovered. That's why it was an amazing discovery when divers found a ship in 1996. It is thought that the ship found by the divers was the *Queen Anne's Revenge*. The ship was discovered off the coast of North Carolina, buried in sand under 20 feet (6.1 m) of water. Divers have recovered three anchors, 21 cannons, a brass bell, and a piece of the ship's **hull**. No real riches have been found because Blackbeard most likely carried off the treasure before the ship sank. However, a very small amount of gold dust was discovered. Studying this ship will help us to better understand the everyday life of these fearsome pirates.

Glossary

aground (uh-GROWND) When something has moved onto the shore or the bottom of a body of water.

betrayed (bee-TRAYD) To have turned against.

booty (BOO-tee) Prizes stolen by force.

foreign (FOR-in) Outside one's own country.

fuses (FYOOZ-ez) Slow-burning objects used to set off shells, bombs, or blasts of gunpowder.

hull (HUL) The main body of a ship.

legends (LEH-jendz) Stories passed down through the years that many people believe.

marooned (muh-ROOND) When someone has been left on a deserted island with no hope of escape.

pardon (PAR-din) The excusing of an offense.

pieces of eight (PEES-es UV AYT) Gold coins, used during the Golden Age of Piracy.

plundering (PLUN-der-ing) Robbing by force.

privateer (pry-vuh-TEER) An armed pirate licensed by the government to attack enemy ships.

ransom (RAN-sum) The demand of pay for the release of someone or something.

terrorized (TER-uh-ryzd) To have filled people with great fear.

Index

Web Sites

To find out more about Blackbeard and piracy, check out these Web sites:
http://blackbeard.eastnet.ecu.edu/qarhist.html
www.teachshole.com